POLITICS TODAY

WHO ARE  LIBERTARIANS

and What Do They Believe In?

Tempra Board

Cavendish Square

New York

Cataloging-in-Publication Data

Names: Board, Tempra.
Title: Who are libertarians and what do they believe in? / Tempra Board.
Description: New York : Cavendish Square Publishing, 2020. | Series: Politics today | Includes glossary and index.
Identifiers: LCCN ISBN 9781502645241 (pbk.) | ISBN 9781502645258 (library bound) | ISBN 9781502645265 (ebook)
Subjects: LCSH: Libertarian Party--Juvenile literature. | United States--Politics and government--Juvenile literature.
Classification: LCC JJK2391.L9 B5546 2020 | DDC 324.273--dc23

Editorial Director: David McNamara
Editor: Erin L. McCoy
Copy Editor: Nathan Heidelberger
Associate Art Director: Alan Sliwinski
Designer: Jessica Nevins
Production Coordinator: Karol Szymczuk
Photo Research: J8 Media

The photographs in this book are used by permission and through the courtesy of: Cover (left column- top to bottom) AXL/Shutterstock.com, Lane V. Erickson/Shutterstock.com, 3dfoto/Shutterstock.com, (right) Andrea Izzotti/Shutterstock.com; p. 4 Sascha Burkard/Shutterstock.com; p. 7 North Wind Picture Archives; p. 8 NYPL/Science Source/Getty Images; p. 9 The Ludwig von Mises Institute/Wikimedia Commons/File:Murray Rothbard.jpg/CC BY SA 3.0; p. 11 Bryan R. Smith/AFP/Getty Images; p. 13 Pew Research Center; p. 14 Matt Winkelmeyer/Getty Images for WIRED25; p. 16 Jeff Malet Photography/Newscom; p. 18 Ludwig von Mises Institute/Wikimedia Commons/File:Ludwig von Mises.jpg/CC BY SA 3.0; p. 20 George Frey/Bloomberg/Getty Images; p. 21 Aaron Haupt/Science Source/Getty Images; p. 22 Social Security Online/Wikimedia Commons/Library of Congress/File:Signing Of The Social Security Act.jpg/Public Domain; p. 25 Bettmann/Getty Images; p. 26 Libertarian Party Logo/Wikia/Logopedia/Libertarian Party US Logo.png; p. 28 Lightspring/Shutterstock.com; p. 30 Photo.ua/Shutterstock.com; p. 33 Hulton Archive/Getty Images; p. 34 Mikhail Kolesnikov/Shutterstock.com; p. 35 Evan Brandt/The Mercury/AP Images; p. 36 Mikhail Kolesnikov/Shutterstock.com; p. 38 Blvdone/Shutterstock.com; p. 40 Chris Ratcliffe/Bloomberg/Getty Images; p. 42 David Bacon/Alamy Stock Photo; p. 44 Samuel Corum/Anadolu Agency/Getty Images; p. 47 Shah Marai/AFP/Getty Images; p. 48 ZUMA Press Inc/Alamy Stock Photo.

Printed in the United States of America

★ Contents

THE ...

held at the City of New ...

of March, one thousand seven hundred ...

ARTICLES in addition to, and amendment of the Constitution ...

We the People

insure domestic Tranquility, provide for the common ...

and our Posterity, do ordain and establish this ...

Chapter 1

What Makes a Libertarian

Libertarianism is a political ideology, or school of thought, that upholds liberty and personal freedom as its main principles. Libertarians believe in the importance of defending the rights of individuals to govern themselves and to make their own choices about their lives. This means that nothing should stand in the way of an individual's ability to pursue life, liberty, and making a living, so long as these pursuits do not harm any other individual's ability to do the same. For libertarians, this means that the government should not interfere in people's lives or their property for any other reason than to protect these freedoms.

Libertarians believe that government should be much smaller than it is today, consisting of simply a justice system and a small military force for protection. Many areas in which the US government currently operates, such as education and health care, would instead be privately operated. There would be no taxes imposed on citizens. Funding of any services would be coordinated and collected voluntarily, or willingly, by the people and not through force by the government.

Opposite: Pictured here is the original preamble to the United States Constitution, written in 1787.

Economics

How the economic system of the United States should function is an important concern for libertarians. They believe that there should be fewer rules governing financial transactions or business dealings. Furthermore, they argue that the capitalist free-market system of economics should be allowed to work without government interference or regulations.

The United States already functions under a capitalist system, which means that trade and industry are controlled by private individuals or companies, not by the government. However, the government currently imposes restrictions and laws on the free market. It also imposes taxes to support government-provided services such as education and the military. We will further explore the economic principles of libertarianism later in this book.

A Brief History of Libertarian Thought

As they worked to outline the fundamental principles by which the United States would operate, the Founding Fathers had personal freedom and liberty very much in mind. In declaring the United States an independent country, they had asserted their freedom from what they saw as the coercive and unfair system of British rule. In what may be the most famous lines of the Declaration of Independence (1776), Thomas Jefferson wrote:

> We hold these truths to be self-evident, that all men are created equal, that they are endowed by their Creator with certain unalienable Rights, that among these are Life, Liberty and the pursuit of Happiness.– That to secure these rights, Governments are instituted among Men, deriving their just powers from the consent of the governed,–That whenever

any Form of Government becomes destructive of these ends, it is the Right of the People to alter or to abolish it, and to institute new Government, laying its foundation on such principles and organizing its powers in such form, as to them shall seem most likely to effect their Safety and Happiness.

However, the ideals of self-governance go back much further than the year 1776. Over the course of several centuries of European history, for example, philosophers and theologians wrote about the freedom to practice one's own religion rather than the one mandated by kings and queens. The ideal of religious freedom came to be seen as a more general freedom from royal, or centralized, power.

During the Middle Ages in Europe, these ideas gained further importance and influence, as seen in documents such as the Magna Carta in England, signed in 1215. The Magna

This woodcut depicts the life of Celtic people who were required to work in servitude to their chieftain during the Middle Ages.

Political philosopher John Locke is pictured circa 1704 in this engraving.

Carta called for not only religious freedom but limits on payments (taxes) to the king, which were required in feudal times.

Libertarian ideas rose to prominence in eighteenth-century Europe, during the Age of Reason, or the Enlightenment period. The political philosopher John Locke wrote that government should exist only to protect people's "natural rights," that is, the rights that people have prior to the existence of government, such as the rights to life and freedom.

Libertarians' strong emphasis on private and personal property may also be rooted in Locke's theories. Locke wrote that everyone has a "property" consisting of his or her own body, and by extension, the work of this body (anything we create or labor on, such as a work of art or a garden we tend). Therefore, land worked by a person also becomes his or her property. This was contrary to the feudal system in which all land was owned by a small number of kings or feudal lords appointed by the monarchy.

Property rights are one of the major concerns of modern libertarians, who believe that people should be free to earn a living by their own hand, and free from government taxes on that income. Similarly, the land one owns should not be taxed, and people should be free to do as they please with and on their property, as long as doing so does not harm others.

We will explore the issue of property rights and how these might affect current needs for environmental protection in a later chapter.

The Austrian School

The modern libertarian movement often cites what is called the Austrian school of economic thought. The Austrian school is named after the country of its founder, Carl Menger, an economist at the University of Vienna. It was popularized by the Austrian writer and economist Ludwig von Mises, who published several influential books and essays in the early to mid-twentieth century.

Mises was a strong critic of socialism, which could be seen as the polar opposite of free-market capitalism. In a socialist system, all goods and services are owned and operated by the community as a whole (via a central governmental body), rather than by private individuals. Mises and others feared that overreaching government power would not only stifle personal liberties but would thwart wealth and prosperity.

In the United States, economist Murray Rothbard further popularized the Austrian school of economics. Rothbard published dozens of

Economist Murray Rothbard popularized the Austrian school of economics.

books on political theory and economics in the mid- to late twentieth century and was a strong advocate of privatization. He believed that government-provided services were inefficient and created a dangerous monopoly, affording the government too much control over the price and distribution of industries, goods, and services.

In his book *For a New Liberty: The Libertarian Manifesto,* Rothbard warns of what he sees as a socialist takeover of individual rights any time a society's rights are given priority over individual rights. "'Society' is sometimes treated as a superior or quasi-divine figure with overriding 'rights' of its own," Rothbard contends. However, he insists that "treating society as a thing that chooses and acts … serves to obscure the real forces at work." Rothbard argues that taxation and laws that limit an individual's rights are fundamentally harmful to the success of individuals and, ultimately, society as a whole.

The Libertarian Party

The Libertarian Party in the United States was founded in late 1971 in Colorado by a group of individuals concerned about the economic policies of then-president Richard Nixon. Among its founders were Rothbard and David Nolan, who served as its chairman for many years.

The Libertarian Party gained some prominence during the 1988 presidential election when former Republican congressman Ron Paul joined the party and ran against George H. W. Bush and Michael Dukakis. Paul had become disillusioned with what he felt was the Republican Party's massive deficit spending, which was increasing the national debt. In the election, Paul came in a distant third place, with less than 1 percent of the popular vote.

Libertarian presidential candidate Gary Johnson (*left*) and vice presidential candidate William Weld are pictured at a rally in New York in 2016.

In modern decades, the Libertarian Party has become a popular alternative to the dominant two-party political system. In 2016, the Libertarian Party's presidential candidate, Gary Johnson, earned 3.28 percent of the popular vote, a record high for the party. While this may not sound like a lot, it represents nearly 4.5 million votes, and may have played a role in the election of Donald J. Trump, who won by an extremely small margin.

Today, the Libertarian Party platform asserts that libertarians "seek a world of liberty: a world in which all individuals are sovereign over their own lives and are not forced to sacrifice their values for the benefit of others." The party outlines a number of its policy positions on the role of government and addresses what it sees as the dangers

The very word "libertarian" has gained prominence in popular culture and in the news over the past several years. Yet it is not always clear that people understand its meaning. A large-scale survey of thousands of people conducted by the Pew Research Center in 2014 found that, although 14 percent of respondents called themselves "libertarian," only 11 percent both called themselves libertarian and could correctly define the term.

The survey found distinct differences according to gender and ethnic background. More than twice as many men (15 percent) as women (7 percent) self-identify as libertarian. Four times as many white Americans (12 percent) say they are libertarian, compared with just 3 percent of African Americans. Libertarians are also more likely to be high-income, with 16 percent of those earning $75,000 per year or more identifying as libertarian, compared with only 7 percent of those earning less than $30,000. Twice as many registered Republicans say that they define themselves as libertarian (12 percent) compared with registered Democrats (6 percent). Among registered independents, 14 percent say they are libertarian.

Pew also found that many Americans hold libertarian views and political values, though they might not call themselves libertarians. Names and labels evolve over time, and can gain positive and negative connotations depending on how they are used. For example, a "feminist" is simply someone who believes that women should have the same rights as men. Yet many people do not want to be called feminists because of the sometimes-negative connotations associated with that word.

The Pew Research Center also asked thousands of people a series of twenty-three questions about social and political values to create a "political typology." Based on this typology, groups of people with the same kinds of responses were clustered into political "types," such as Steadfast Conservatives, Business Conservatives, Solid Liberals, Young Outsiders, and Faith and Family Left. The results of this study showed that not all Republicans are the same, and that the same can be said for Democrats.

The groupings can also tell us something about libertarians. The group with the largest percentage of self-identified libertarians was Business Conservatives. In this group, you might expect to find the CEOs of large corporations. More than one in four (27 percent) Business Conservatives support limited government, particularly when it comes to how government affects business. In a later chapter, we will discuss why large corporations may favor libertarian policies, and what that means for businesses and individuals.

Men	15%
Women	7%
White	12%
African American	3%
Earn above $75,000	16%
Earn below $30,000	7%
Republican	12%
Democrat	6%
Independent	14%

In 2014, the Pew Research Center determined the demographics of those Americans who self-identified as libertarians.

of government's overreach. The platform also outlines the party's positions on everything from privacy laws, to how we should address crime, to the rules governing economics and the marketplace, to national defense. We will discuss these stances in more detail in future chapters.

Prominent Libertarians

Libertarianism as a school of thought began with economists and political theorists, but libertarians can be found everywhere in our society, including among writers, entertainers, corporate executives, and politicians. Jeff Bezos, CEO of Amazon (and as of 2018, the richest person in the world, with a net worth of $166 billion), has been described by some as a libertarian. David Koch, co-owner of the enormous multinational corporation Koch Industries with his brother Charles, is also a libertarian. The Koch brothers

Jeff Bezos, founder of online retail company Amazon, speaks at a San Francisco, California, summit in 2018.

are known for their sizable funding of conservative political candidates and support for economic policies that favor big business. Right-wing radio talk-show host Glenn Beck is a libertarian, as are the actors Clint Eastwood, Gary Oldman, and Vince Vaughn.

The popular television show *Parks and Recreation* satirized a stereotype of libertarians in the fictional character of Parks Department director Ron Swanson (played by actor Nick Offerman), who comically wanted to abolish the very department that he oversaw. Many modern libertarians indeed advocate for the abolishment of such government agencies as the Department of Education and the Environmental Protection Agency. The next chapter goes into more detail regarding the libertarian perspective on the role of government and politics in our daily lives.

★ Chapter 2

Politics and Government

Libertarians believe that government should be limited. But what does this mean in practice? How limited should it be? Do libertarians believe there should be no government at all? As we will see in this chapter, the answer is not always simple, and many libertarians disagree about how small the government should be.

The Role of Government

Taken at its most basic level, libertarian ideology proposes that government in its current form should cease to exist. This is because libertarians see many of our current laws as infringements on personal freedom and liberty. An example would be the legal requirement that a family must ensure that its children be educated according to certain standards. Libertarians believe that a decision like this should be left up to the family.

Libertarians are strongly opposed to involuntary taxation, especially for what they contend are inefficient, poorly run,

Opposite: A Tea Party activist is pictured at a 2010 protest on tax day in Washington, DC.

Ludwig von Mises was a leading economist from the Austrian school.

and unnecessary government-provided services. The modern Libertarian Party platform denies the government's right to infringe in any way on personal liberties or freedoms.

Ludwig von Mises of the Austrian school of economics was primarily concerned with government's role in economics.

Mises claimed that government regulation and control of economic systems was inefficient. He went further, claiming that government bureaucracy not only is bad for business but is a threat to democracy itself.

The idea that government is inherently inefficient has, in fact, been woven into the collective thinking of the broader culture—so much so that the very word "bureaucracy" has come to have a negative connotation. It is often equated with being wasteful and providing substandard service. However, a bureaucracy is simply a system in which decisions are made by a group of nonelected government officials. In fact, any large system in which a group of individuals makes decisions together is a bureaucracy.

Murray Rothbard claimed that, beyond being inefficient, government amounted to systematic robbery of citizens. Writing in 1973, Rothbard asked, "What is the State anyway but organized banditry? What is taxation but theft on a gigantic, unchecked, scale?" The state, in this instance, refers to any centralized form of government. In the libertarian's ideal world, the Internal Revenue Service—the government agency charged with collecting taxes—would not exist. Under a libertarian system, most government-run programs also would not exist. Therefore, in theory, there would be no need to tax citizens in order to operate these programs.

Today, libertarians continue to be concerned that the United States government and its laws are overreaching and in direct conflict with individual rights. Some point to the heightened security in the United States after the terrorist attacks on September 11, 2001. The United States established the Department of Homeland Security in 2002 and initiated intensive screening of passengers at airports. You might not remember a time when you were allowed to keep your shoes

A TSA screening agent searches a bag at the Salt Lake City International Airport in 2016.

on as you entered airport security. Before the 9/11 attacks, however, you could do just that.

In an attempt to ramp up security after 9/11, the government also relaxed laws related to individual privacy. For example, it is easier now for the government to obtain any individual's phone and email records. Many people in the United States—and not just libertarians—are concerned that these laws might be too invasive of our privacy. A citizen's right to privacy is protected under the Fourth Amendment to the US Constitution, which guarantees "[t]he right of the people to be secure in their persons, houses, papers, and effects, against unreasonable searches and seizures."

Interpreting the Constitution

People often disagree about how the United States Constitution should be interpreted. At the time the

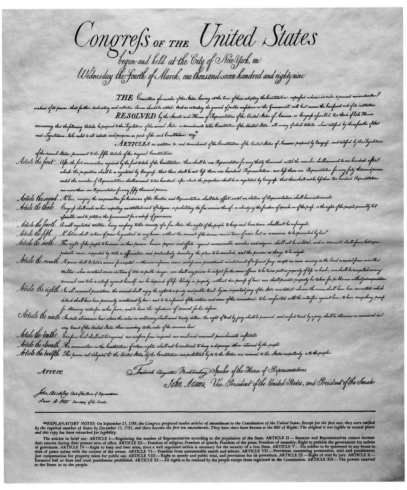

The Bill of Rights, pictured here, outlines specific freedoms and protections for Americans.

Constitution was written in the late eighteenth century, there was no way for the Founding Fathers to anticipate all of the questions that would need legal resolution in the future. Some libertarians cite the Constitution as the ultimate guide to preserving personal freedom. Others claim that it does not go far enough in ensuring that these freedoms are protected.

It is indisputable, however, that the Founding Fathers were committed to limiting the powers of government. For this

Some libertarians claim that the Supreme Court has restricted personal liberties in its interpretation of the Constitution. What many people have called a progressive era in United States politics under President Franklin Delano Roosevelt, between 1933 and 1945, saw a number of key decisions. One was to uphold the Social Security Act.

The Social Security Act was passed in 1935 to address a nationwide problem. Many older adults, once they retired

President Franklin D. Roosevelt signs the Social Security Act in 1935.

or if they were laid off from work, would find themselves without sufficient savings or income and thus would fall into poverty. The Social Security Act ensured that most American seniors would receive a regular social-security stipend to help them pay for food and other daily necessities. Such stipends are funded by regular contributions (in the form of taxes) that American workers and employers make into the social security system.

Shortly after it was passed, the Social Security Act was legally challenged by the Edison Electric Illuminating Company on the grounds that it was unconstitutional to require the company to pay into the Social Security Fund. The case went to the Supreme Court.

In a 7–2 decision, the court decided in 1937 that Social Security was constitutional because the Constitution grants the federal government the right to impose taxes for any purpose that is deemed to be for the "general welfare" of the United States. The court agreed that the plight of older adults clearly fell into that category.

Many libertarians disagree with this ruling, often on the grounds that federal taxation for this purpose violates states' rights as outlined in the Tenth Amendment.

reason, they set up three branches of government in order to restrict the reach of any one branch. These are the executive branch, which includes the president, vice president, the president's cabinet, and various federal agencies; the legislative branch, or Congress; and the judicial branch, comprised of the Supreme Court and lower courts. The Founding Fathers also divided power between the federal government and the states. Finally, they protected the civil liberties of American citizens through the Bill of Rights, a list of ten amendments to the Constitution.

The United States Supreme Court is charged with interpreting the Constitution, including the Bill of Rights. The Supreme Court's decisions form precedents—or standards that are then used by the Supreme Court and lower courts in deciding future cases on similar issues. The Constitution, as interpreted by the Supreme Court, has served to both protect and take away personal freedoms.

Libertarians generally acknowledge that the Constitution has worked in favor of personal freedom. Libertarian legal scholar Randy E. Barnett, delivering a presentation at Georgetown University Law Center in 2008, stated:

> Few can point to other countries where individuals are freer in practice than in the U.S. Many libertarians might be willing to move there, if such a place existed; yet no such exodus has occurred. And in important respects, life as an American feels freer than it once did. We seem to have more choices than ever before, and are freer to live the sorts of lives we wish. Libertarians still refer to the U.S. as a "free country," maybe still the freest on earth … That the Constitution deserves at least some of the credit for this freedom seems likely.

In 1937, the US Supreme Court, pictured here in 1935, ruled in a 7-2 decision that the Social Security Act was constitutional.

Laws and Justice

A literal interpretation of libertarianism might lead one to conclude that libertarians oppose all forms of government, making them essentially anarchists. There are, indeed, some schools of libertarian thought that argue for a more anarchic society. However, most influential libertarians argue that they are not anarchists—rather, they do support some limited laws and powers of government—specifically those laws that protect individual freedoms. David Boaz, in *Libertarianism: A Primer*, imagines such a minimal government in this way:

Individuals have the right to do whatever they want to, so long as they respect the equal rights of others. The role of government is to protect individual rights from foreign aggressors and from neighbors who murder, rape, rob, assault, or defraud us. And if government seeks to do more than that, it will itself be depriving us of our rights and liberties.

What does this mean with respect to modern-day laws and civil liberties? Which laws do libertarians believe are just, and which do they think should be abolished as infringing too much on our rights?

The 2018 Libertarian Party platform lays out its stances on a variety of issues. It addresses the right to free speech and expression, claiming that any government control over media or technology is a violation of this right. The

party also strongly supports the right to privacy and freedom from government spying, and opposes the death penalty. It opposes military intervention in other countries, adding that the "only legitimate use of force is in defense of individual rights—life, liberty, and justly acquired property—against aggression."

As we have described above, a free and open economic marketplace is one of the Libertarian Party's main focuses. There should be no government restrictions to an individual or corporation's property rights so long as they do not harm the rights of others. As we will see in an

The 2018 Libertarian Party logo shows a torch with a flame shaped like an eagle.

upcoming chapter, this issue becomes thorny as we attempt to determine what actions on one person's or corporation's property might constitute harm to others.

With regard to economics, the Libertarian Party believes the government should never go into debt, because such debt, which must be repaid in the future, places a financial burden on "future generations without their consent."

Similarly, the party does not support government intrusion into lending practices. For example, our government currently guarantees student loan debt. Student loans, which many people use who would not otherwise be able to afford to go to college, are currently treated differently in bankruptcy proceedings than other types of debt. This means that if a borrower defaults—or is unable to repay—a student loan and files for bankruptcy, the federal government will step in and repay the lender. The Libertarian Party argues that such government intrusion into lending should end because it places a burden on the public to pay (through their taxes) a government bailout to lending companies.

The Libertarian Party states that health care should be provided under a free-market system, which would mean the elimination of government-supported care such as Medicare for older adults and Medicaid for people with low incomes. The party also favors bringing an end to Social Security in favor of a private, voluntary system of investment. In such a system, any support for retired people with no income would become the responsibility of charitable organizations and individuals in a voluntary manner and would not be funded through government taxes.

The Libertarian Party also addresses social issues. As of 2018, the party was pro-choice, with the understanding that every woman—rather than the government—should have control over her own body. Some prominent libertarians, however, disagree with this thinking. Most notable among them is Ron Paul, who states that in his view, abortion is a violent act against another person. This argument assumes that the unborn fetus—at any time in its development in the womb—is a "person" with the same rights any person should have. The Supreme Court's ruling in *Roe v. Wade*, however, found that this is not the case.

Participation in Government

Civic engagement, or participation by the public, includes actions such as voting, one of our most fundamental rights as citizens of a democracy. Civic engagement can also involve other actions people take individually or collectively with

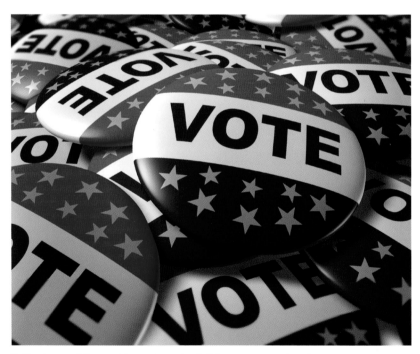

Voting is one of the most important acts of civic engagement in a democracy.

others, such as volunteering; organizing around a particular policy issue that is important to you and educating your friends and neighbors about it; or helping a candidate get elected. Civic participation is considered by many to be essential for a contributing member of society.

Libertarian thinkers, with their strongly held distrust of government and its institutions, are split on the question of whether or how much we should be involved in civics. One argument is that any civic engagement, such as the act of voting, is inherently supportive of government and its laws, many of which are seen as threatening to personal liberties and freedoms. Two prominent libertarian thinkers from the nineteenth century, Benjamin Tucker and Lysander Spooner, believed that voting amounted to a moral wrong. By participating at all in the system of government and its regulations, voters are voicing their support for the system itself. These thinkers believed that the proper role of libertarians should be to actively fight against the systems of government oppression.

Ron Paul, in his book *Liberty Defined: 50 Essential Issues That Affect Our Freedom,* argues that the very system of democracy, in which a simple 51 percent majority decides laws and who gets elected, is problematic. He states that "people should not be able to vote to take away the rights of others," adding that any law that passes with a small margin is ultimately suppressing the wishes of the large minority of people who voted against it. Even so, Paul agrees that democratic elections can be used to promote leaders who will uphold liberties, and many other libertarians agree. Others believe that striving to educate the public about the virtues of libertarian ideals is a more useful path than voting. Such efforts are themselves another form of civic engagement.

Chapter 3

Libertarian Ideology and Economics

Libertarian ideology is highly concerned with economics, as one of its major platforms is the importance of the free-market system. To gain a deeper understanding of this ideology, let's first take a look at various types of economic systems in use throughout the world and the government's role in each.

Types of Economic Systems

Economies throughout the world can be categorized into four basic types: traditional, command, market, and mixed.

In traditional economies—common in many developing countries with large rural populations—the economy is defined by the beliefs, customs, and traditions of its people. Rather than the specialization and division of labor found in other types of economies, most people survive by subsistence farming (raising their own food) or other small-scale farming and business enterprises.

Command economies, sometimes referred to as "planned economies," exist when one entity—the government—controls

Opposite: The New York Stock Exchange building on Wall Street in New York City is pictured in 2015. This is one of the financial centers of the United States.

a large part of all goods and services, as well as most natural resources. This is most often found in communist countries. China and North Korea are examples of communist governments and command economies.

A market economic system is one in which all economic activity is regulated directly by the people and through the process of supply and demand, with no government interference or regulation. A truly market-based system exists only in theory, as there is no economic system anywhere in the world that is completely absent of government regulation.

A mixed economic system, also called a "dual economic system," is a combination of a command economy and a market economy. This is the most common economic system in developed countries such as the United States. In most economies, most goods and services are privately owned, with some government regulations (such as anti-monopoly laws) to ensure fairness in the system, as well as some services (such as public benefits like highway maintenance or health care) that are provided and controlled by the government.

The Ideal of Economic Liberty

Libertarians believe that the United States should operate on as free an economic system as possible, meaning that all goods and services would be privately owned and operated, rather than owned and regulated by the government. According to this theory, such an economic system would allow anyone in our society to have the freedom to pursue and achieve economic success. In addition, libertarians argue, if left alone, the free-market process of supply and demand will ensure that everyone can obtain the goods and services they want and need at competitive prices.

Scottish economist and philosopher Adam Smith discusses the libertarian ideals of the free market in his

Economist and philosopher Adam Smith is pictured circa 1765.

groundbreaking *Wealth of Nations,* published in 1776. The book is seen by many as the foundation of modern economics. Smith writes that the free-market system would ultimately lead to benevolence and would benefit humankind. This is because, in order for a person to successfully sell a

The protection of property rights makes good sense on its face. We all want to have control over what we can do in our own homes or on our own land. But what happens when what we want to do impacts others?

The Libertarian Party platform of 2018 states that "Libertarians would free property owners from government restrictions on their rights to control and enjoy their property, as long as their choices do not harm or infringe on the rights of others." Among those restrictions that many libertarians want to eliminate are the limitations placed on such economic activity as logging on some private land.

In many states, logging companies must file timber-harvest plans with state forestry departments before they can begin logging a particular tract of land. These plans outline the number of trees to be cut, the amount of board feet of timber to be harvested, how and where the trees are cut, and how wildlife habitat and water quality will be protected.

Trees and their root systems keep soil in place. When they are removed, runoff of topsoil and even detrimental landslides can occur. This could harm the delicate balance of water quality in the watershed, affecting not only fish and wildlife but also neighbors who might rely on the watershed for their drinking water. Therefore, environmental rules and regulations have been put in place to govern the harvest of timber and try to mitigate these outcomes. Environmentalists argue that if these regulations are lifted, timber-harvest practices could cause severe damage to the environment.

Libertarians argue that any timber company would naturally want to protect its property and investment from negative consequences and would therefore voluntarily follow a set of guidelines to ensure its lands remain healthy and productive, or pay court-ordered restitution for damages done. An unfortunate reality, however, is that it can be extremely difficult for private individuals of limited financial

Landowner Gary Westlake Sr. claims his logging operation is being illegally restricted by a town ordinance.

means to succeed in expensive court cases against very wealthy corporations.

Logging can also cause broader harm to the environment and the climate. Trees remove carbon dioxide from the atmosphere and store it within their living mass. The harvesting of trees releases carbon dioxide into the atmosphere, intensifying global warming.

The Libertarian Party of California, like many other party branches, advocates the "privatization of government-held lands, including parks and beaches." If we were to eliminate government-owned lands—for example, national parks such as Yellowstone and Yosemite—such lands could be sold to private individuals or companies to do with as they saw fit. These entities might keep the parks open for the benefit of anyone to visit and enjoy. However, private owners could also choose to close the parks entirely to exploit their natural resources through logging, mining, or other development.

Yosemite National Park is a federally protected area where logging is generally prohibited in order to preserve the natural environment.

product or service, he or she must provide something that others need and will benefit from at a price they are willing to pay. For example, a manufacturer will not be successful charging $400 for a tablet or e-reader if another company can provide the same features and the same quality tablet at $100. The competitive market will therefore adjust itself if left alone, through the simple systems of supply and demand and market competition.

In addition, libertarians believe that an open and free economy will drive more innovation than one that is controlled by the government. Many cite the example of the Enlightenment period in Europe, during which economies, art, and culture flourished within the context of a strong push by popular thinkers for laissez-faire economics (literally translated from the French as "let us do").

Although libertarians support a market-based system of economics, most also agree that there must be at least some laws and regulations to protect people from fraud, defend their property rights, and settle disputes. However, anything more than this is seen as government overreach and as an affront to personal liberties. This includes government restrictions on an individual's private property and on his or her ability to make as much profit as possible from such property, provided it does not infringe on anyone else's rights. Libertarians might also be opposed to government control over goods and services such as the provision of health services, education, or transportation.

The Role of Money in Financial Markets

Economies are controlled by each country's central bank—a government-run entity that oversees the production and distribution of money and credit. The central bank of the United States is called the Federal Reserve. The Federal Reserve manages the US money supply by establishing and implementing monetary policy.

One way that central banks influence the economy is by trying to control inflation, which is the increase in the price of goods and services over time. For example, in 1950, you could purchase a new car for around $2,000. Today, you might have trouble finding one for $20,000. The average rate of inflation between 1950 and 2018 was 2.28 percent per year, meaning that $100 in 1950 had the same purchasing power as nearly $1,050 now. A central bank might try to control inflation by setting interest rates or by regulating the printing of currency.

Setting the federal funds interest rate—which is the amount that banks can charge other banks to borrow

The US Federal Reserve building is in Washington, DC. The Federal Reserve manages monetary policy within the United States.

money for their reserves—is a key responsibility of most central banks. In the United States, banks use their reserves to invest in large-scale projects and to support other kinds of lending. When the Federal Reserve raises the federal funds rate, it discourages such borrowing. When it lowers it, more borrowing is encouraged, which makes more money available to the economy. A lower federal funds rate can encourage investment in property and home buying, as large purchases and loans are dramatically affected by even a small interest-rate change.

Another means of controlling the economy—and the rate of inflation—is through regulating the printing of currency. Only the central bank of a country can print more money, and doing so can have significant economic consequences. If the money supply increases too quickly, it speeds up inflation, making goods more expensive for consumers and investors, and potentially resulting in an economic slowdown or even a recession.

A Libertarian View of Monetary Policy

Libertarians are concerned with what they see as our government's tendency to engage in what is called expansionary monetary policy. Expansionary monetary policy adds more money to the economy, usually by encouraging increased lending (in part through lower interest rates, as we discussed above) or by printing more money. In contrast, contractionary monetary policy reduces the amount of money in the economy.

The prominent libertarian Ron Paul claims that expansionary monetary policy has occurred because money is no longer rooted in such commodities as gold and silver. (Basing money on gold is called the "gold standard.") He claims that once the United States started printing more money, it created economic instability in the form of "boom and bust" economic cycles.

Paul, along with many other libertarians, also believes that the federal government's control over the monetary system, especially through its guarantee of loans, creates instability and economic danger. In *Liberty Defined,* Paul argues that the current US monetary system "guarantees that investors and banks will push the envelope and make careless speculative decisions that generate a bubble economy waiting to burst."

Some libertarians argue that basing money on the gold standard would increase economic stability.

For example, when some of the big banks began failing in 2008 as a result of the housing-market crisis and ensuing recession, the government bailed them out. Many libertarians insisted that US taxpayers were unfairly paying the price for a federally controlled economic and monetary system.

Who Benefits from a Libertarian Economic System?

It's no coincidence that, as we discussed earlier, many prominent businesspeople and leaders of large corporations are proponents of libertarian thought. Many entrepreneurs from such places as California's Silicon Valley—the heart of the American tech industry—advocate less government intrusion in big business. Greater market freedoms and fewer government restrictions will theoretically result in larger profits for businesses. Large businesses that gain political power through lobbying and political campaign spending can help to get laws passed (or repealed) that will allow them to earn more money.

Is this a bad thing? It may depend where the line is drawn with respect to government intervention. For example, most Americans would agree that laws restricting child labor are a good thing. But what about the minimum wage? A libertarian argument for abolishing the minimum-wage requirement insists that a free market would equalize wages because companies could not pay less than what people would be willing to work for. However, some argue that this is too simplistic. In many parts of the United States where the unemployment rate is high, people may be forced to work for wages that are unfairly low.

★ Chapter 4

Social and Cultural Issues

Libertarians are not just concerned with economic issues. Many laws and policies can have an impact on cultural and religious beliefs and practices. As described earlier in this book, libertarian ideas arose in part out of the desire for religious freedom. According to libertarian ideology, each individual should have the freedom to make personal and professional decisions based on their cultural and religious practices. This right should not be impeded by anyone, least of all by the government.

Freedom of Religion

The Libertarian Party maintains that people should be free to "engage in or abstain from any religious activities that do not violate the rights of others." It places freedom of religion in the same category as freedom of speech, maintaining, as in the Constitution, that both should be protected.

The matter of freedom of religion has become a controversial issue in the last few decades, especially for businesses. Some business owners argue that they should

Opposite: People pick up necessities at a food bank in rural Hollister, California, in 2011.

Muslims pray in a mosque in Washington in 2016. Freedom of religion is supported by the Libertarian Party and protected by the US Bill of Rights.

not be required to provide certain services or benefits to their employees or to potential customers if doing so would violate their religious beliefs.

The argument over religious freedom has led to fierce debate regarding workplace discrimination. For example, imagine that a large company, which offers health insurance to its employees, is owned by a devout Christian who does not believe in birth control. Can the owner of this company refuse to provide health insurance that covers birth control?

This question was brought before the Supreme Court in 2014 in the case of *Burwell v. Hobby Lobby Stores*. In a 5-4 decision, the court concluded that Hobby Lobby, which is owned by a family of Christians who believe birth control is immoral, could deny contraception coverage to its employees as allowed by the Religious Freedom Restoration Act.

Addressing Discrimination

Some people worry that calls for religious freedom could result in other kinds of discrimination, for example against members of the lesbian, gay, bisexual, transgender, and queer (LGBTQ) community. Because many people hold that being anything but heterosexual is wrong according to their religious beliefs, they might choose not to provide services or jobs to LGBTQ people—an act of discrimination which, in many states and contexts in the United States, is illegal. Hate crimes against people based on their sexual orientation, perceived or actual gender, or gender identity, were outlawed in 2009 with the passage of the Matthew Shepard and James Byrd, Jr. Hate Crimes Prevention Act.

Prominent libertarian thinkers such as Ron Paul make the case that discrimination should not be legislated by the government. He believes that the special definition of "hate crimes" should be abolished, because it allows the government to punish crimes differently based on the motivation for the crime (a subjective assessment) and whom it has been perpetrated against. He calls this another form of discrimination based on group identity.

In *The Libertarian Manifesto*, Murray Rothbard argues that conservatives and liberals seek to impose their specific morality onto others, which is incompatible with libertarian thought. The Libertarian Party platform states simply that the government should have no involvement in the personal relationships of people, which includes definitions of marriage and issues of gender and gender identity.

Early libertarian thinkers admonished slavery and believed in the natural rights of all humans, including women and people of color. For hundreds of years in the United States, these groups did not have the right to vote or own property, and indeed were actually considered the property of white men.

However, modern-day libertarians may bristle at the idea of any law that attempts to "right the wrongs" of the past and to level the playing field for marginalized communities who are still at a disadvantage in society. Some are especially critical of affirmative action, policies that governments, schools, and companies adopt to help address inequalities in areas such as employment, pay rates, and education for minority groups that have suffered from discrimination. In many libertarians' minds, affirmative action is nothing but discrimination of another sort. They insist that the answer to addressing discrimination in business practices would be a free-market solution that involves boycotting and shaming discriminatory companies.

National Security, International Affairs, and Immigration

The best method for securing the United States' national borders is a source of much ongoing political debate. How do the libertarian ideals of life and liberty relate to issues of foreign aid and aggression, domestic security, and the movement of people between countries?

Waging War

Modern-day libertarians are strongly opposed to war. This opposition is based on the fundamental belief that the government has no right to use coercion or force against any individual or group, an act that in and of itself hampers freedom and liberty. Although a nation may retaliate against another nation to defend against aggression, it may not do so in a manner that may cause innocent lives to be lost. Civilian casualties are nearly always a cost of war. Murray Rothbard,

A US soldier is pictured at the Kandahar military base in Afghanistan in 2018.

writing in 1963, argued particularly against the use and development of nuclear weapons due to the indiscriminate mass destruction they have the potential to cause.

The modern Libertarian Party calls for the "principle of non-initiation of force" in guiding government relationships between nations. The party supports a military force only large enough to defend the United States from foreign aggression.

Libertarians believe that it is not the responsibility of the government to provide social programs, whether they support basic needs—such as food and housing—or help bring people out of poverty, such as offsetting the costs of a college education. Libertarians believe that, although these are noble goals, they should not be compulsory—in other words, we should not be required to provide these benefits through our tax dollars. Instead, these programs should be voluntarily funded. Private entities, such as religious and nonprofit organizations—often called charitable organizations or charities—should provide these benefits.

Homeless families receive a Christmas dinner in Modesto, California, in 2010. Libertarians argue that it is not the government's job to provide such social services as food aid to those in need.

There are thousands of such organizations in the United States. According to Giving USA, individuals and corporations donated $410.2 billion to these charities in 2018, which is equal to 2.9 percent of the United States' GDP (gross domestic product—the total value of goods and services produced in the United States). These charities provide aid of all types, including health services, feeding programs, housing assistance, education and workforce training, and youth programs, to people throughout the United States and the world.

If the government no longer funded programs such as Social Security and health care, could these charities handle the burden? One theory is that the free market, if left alone, would help to improve the livelihoods of more people, leaving fewer people in need of help. Another theory is that, without government support, people's personal goodwill and desire to help would naturally fill the gap. This theory has not been tested in the United States. Some worry that there would not be enough privately supported charity to help people who are impoverished, unemployed, or disabled, and who are at risk of homelessness and starvation.

It also opposes the draft—or compulsory (required) military service.

Similar to the belief that government should not be involved in assistance programs for people in the United States who are poor or otherwise disadvantaged, libertarians also do not generally support the waging of wars for any humanitarian reason. They argue that federal tax dollars should not be used for wars, or for any purpose outside the United States, including for humanitarian aid to other countries.

Another argument against war is that it is often used for political gain and results in increased governmental power. Politicians have used wars in the past to rally Americans to a single cause, bringing the country together and thereby enabling Congress to easily allocate funding to military efforts. After Social Security and unemployment benefits (which are paid for by employers and employees) and health care, the military is the next-largest spending category in the federal budget.

Free Trade and Immigration

Many libertarians believe in free trade between countries and in the unimpeded or unconstrained migration of individuals across political boundaries. The modern Libertarian Party platform states that "economic freedom demands the unrestricted movement of human as well as financial capital across national borders."

Some libertarians assert that if the free market were allowed to function, our economy would be stronger and the need for labor would increase, meaning that there would be plenty of jobs to go around for US citizens and newly arrived immigrants alike. Some have advocated for a more permissive "worker status" for people who have come to this country illegally. Others, though, including Ron Paul, have taken a very different stance, insisting that we should not automatically grant birthright citizenship to children born in the United States to parents who are undocumented immigrants.

There are also libertarians who disagree with the concept of an open border. They cite the protection of collective property rights (land in the United States that is publicly owned) as one reason, and see undocumented immigrants as potential trespassers on such lands. Some also claim that the United States should have a greater obligation to its own citizens than to noncitizens. They may see immigration as a threat to citizens whose jobs may be taken away or whose tax dollars could go toward providing immigrants public benefits and resources. Similar to the argument against engaging in foreign aid, this reasoning says that we should not aid people from other countries, even if they are coming here to escape dire circumstances in their home countries.

The United States was founded on the governing documents of the Constitution and Bill of Rights, which set up a foundation for the protection of all United States citizens within a democratic republic. The best way to interpret and adapt these documents to best serve the people will continue to be a source of debate among scholars and politicians. The libertarian school of thought and the Libertarian Party provide a unique set of viewpoints that distinguish them from the two dominant political parties of the United States—Democrats and Republicans. Despite falling outside the two-party system, the libertarian ideology nonetheless remains influential in the political sphere today.

Chronology

1215 The Magna Carta is agreed to by King John of England.

1685 The Age of Reason, or the Enlightenment period, begins in Europe. It will last until around 1815.

1776 Adam Smith publishes *An Inquiry into the Nature and Causes of the Wealth of Nations* in Scotland.

1776 The Declaration of Independence is adopted in the United States.

1788 The United States Constitution is ratified, or agreed to, by the majority of US states.

1791 The first ten Constitutional amendments, or the Bill of Rights, are ratified.

1871 The Austrian school of economics is founded.

1935 President Franklin D. Roosevelt signs the Social Security Act into law.

1937 The US Supreme Court hears a challenge against the Social Security Act and votes to uphold it.

1971 The Libertarian Party of the United States is founded.

1973 Murray Rothbard publishes *For a New Liberty: The Libertarian Manifesto*.

1988 Ron Paul gains prominence as the Libertarian Party candidate for US president.

2002 The Department of Homeland Security is formed following the attacks of September 11, 2001.

2011 Ron Paul publishes *Liberty Defined: 50 Essential Issues That Affect Our Freedom*.

2012 Gary Johnson runs for president as the Libertarian Party candidate for the first time. He will run again in 2016.

2014 The Pew Research Center finds that 11 percent of Americans identify as libertarian.

Age of Reason Also called the Enlightenment, a seventeenth- and eighteenth-century political and philosophical movement in Europe promoting the importance of reason, liberty, and science over traditional and religious orthodoxy.

anarchist A person who supports a complete absence of government or authority.

Austrian school of economics A school of economic thought originating in Vienna, Austria, in the late nineteenth century that promoted limited government control over economic matters.

Bill of Rights The first ten amendments to the United States Constitution.

bureaucracy Any large system in which a group of individuals makes decisions together.

capitalism An economic and political system in which a country's trade and industry are largely controlled by private owners, instead of by the government.

central bank The monetary authority of a country that manages its currency, money supply, and interest rates.

civic engagement Political and nonpolitical processes and efforts that seek to improve life in a community.

command economy Also called a planned economy, a system in which one entity—the government—controls a large part of a country's trade and industry.

connotation The secondary or associated meaning of a word or phrase.

conservative A political ideology that seeks to preserve traditional values.

Constitution of the United States The supreme law of the United States.

Declaration of Independence A statement adopted in Philadelphia on July 4, 1776, that the thirteen American colonies would regard themselves as a sovereign state, independent from British rule.

democracy A system of government by all of the people, typically through elected government representation.

entrepreneur A person who owns or operates a business, typically taking financial risks to do so.

Federal Reserve The central banking system of the United States.

feminist Someone who believes that women should have equal rights to men.

free-market economics A system in which the price for goods and services is determined by consumers through supply and demand, without government intervention.

free trade International trade without restrictions.

gold standard A monetary system in which the value of currency is defined in terms of gold, for which the currency can be exchanged.

inflation An increase in prices and a decrease in the value of money.

laissez-faire economics An economic system in which transactions between private parties are free from government intervention such as regulation, privileges, tariffs, and subsidies.

liberal A political ideology that supports social and political equality and change.

libertarian Someone who upholds liberty, or freedom, as a core value. In political terms, someone who also believes in limited government.

Magna Carta A charter of rights agreed to by King John of England in 1215; a symbol of liberty that influenced the Founding Fathers of the United States.

market economy An economic system in which all economic activity is regulated directly by the people and through the process of supply and demand with no government interference or regulation.

mixed economy Also called a dual economy, a combination of a command economy and a market economy.

monetary policy The process by which a country's money is controlled, typically through a central bank or currency board.

monopoly The exclusive control of the supply or trade in a commodity or service by one entity.

recession A slowdown in a country's economic activity.

republic A government run by the people through their elected representatives, led by an elected or nominated president or leader.

socialism A political and economic system in which all goods and services are owned and operated by the community as a whole via the government.

supply and demand An economic force in which a product, commodity, or service and its price and availability are determined by the desire of buyers.

theologian Someone who studies the nature of God and religions.

traditional economy An economy that is defined by the beliefs, customs, and traditions of its people.

undocumented immigrant A foreign national who resides in the United States illegally.

Books

Barksdale, Aaron, and Joshua Hardy. *Libertarianism in a Nutshell*. Hurley, MS: Broken Press Publications, 2016.

Boaz, David. *The Libertarian Mind: A Manifesto for Freedom*. New York: Simon & Schuster, 2015.

Huemer, Michael. *The Problem of Political Authority: An Examination of the Right to Coerce and the Duty to Obey*. New York: Palgrave Macmillan, 2013.

Paul, Ron. *Liberty Defined: 50 Essential Issues That Affect Our Freedom*. New York: Grand Central Publishing, 2011.

Seavey, Todd. *Libertarianism for Beginners*. Danbury, CT: For Beginners LLC, 2016.

Websites

Foundation for Economic Education
https://fee.org
FEE is a nonprofit education organization that seeks to make libertarian concepts "familiar, credible, and compelling to the rising generation."

"Libertarianism" (Britannica)
https://www.britannica.com/topic/libertarianism-politics
This entry in the online *Encyclopedia Britannica* provides an overview of the basic tenets of libertarian thought from a historical perspective. It is written by David Boaz, a prominent libertarian thinker and leader the Cato Institute, a libertarian think tank.

Stanford Encyclopedia of Philosophy
https://plato.stanford.edu/entries/libertarianism
The entry for libertarianism on the *Stanford Encyclopedia of Philosophy* provides a detailed, nonpartisan definition of libertarian philosophy and thought. The *Stanford Encyclopedia* is a continuously updated reference source on philosophy and related concepts.

Videos

Libertarianism 101
https://www.theadvocates.org/libertarianism-101
The founder of the Advocates for Self-Government, a nonprofit organization dedicated to promoting the ideals of liberty and libertarianism, provides a definition of libertarianism in this hour-long lecture.

Take It to the Limits: Milton Friedman on Libertarianism
https://www.youtube.com/watch?v=JSumJxQ5oy4
In this 1999 interview with Milton Friedman, a senior research fellow at the Hoover Institution and a Nobel laureate in economic sciences, Friedman defines the libertarian movement and how smaller government can be balanced with issues of environmental and public safety.

What It Means to Be a Libertarian
https://theihs.org/who-we-are/what-is-libertarian
In this two-minute video, Jeff Miron, a professor of economics at Harvard University, explains the basic foundation of what it means to be a libertarian, and why he believes libertarians are fundamentally different from conservatives or liberals.

Barnett, Randy. "Is the Constitution Libertarian?" Georgetown Public Law and Legal Theory Research Paper No. 1432854, Georgetown Law Library, 2009.

Beam, Christopher. "The Trouble with Liberty." *New York Magazine*, December 26, 2010. http://nymag.com/news/politics/70282.

"Beyond Red vs. Blue: The Political Typology." Pew Research Center, 2014. http://www.people-press.org/2014/06/26/the-political-typology-beyond-red-vs-blue.

Boaz, David. *Libertarianism: A Primer.* New York: Simon & Schuster Inc., 1997.

"Burwell v. Hobby Lobby Stores." Oyez. Accessed December 10, 2018. https://www.oyez.org/cases/2013/13-354.

D'Amato, David S. "Libertarian Perspectives on Voting." Libertarianism.org, 2018. https://www.libertarianism.org/columns/libertarian-perspectives-voting.

Denson, John V., ed. *Reassessing the Presidency: The Rise of the Executive State and the Decline of Freedom.* Auburn, AL: Ludwig von Mises Institute, 2001.

Hoppe, Hans-Herman, ed. *The Myth of Defense: Essays on the Theory and History of Security.* Auburn, AL: Ludwig von Mises Institute, 2003.

"Introduction to the Major Writings of Ludwig von Mises." Online Library of Liberty. Accessed September 21, 2018. http://oll.libertyfund.org/pages/mises-major-writings.

Kiley, Jocelyn. "In Search of Libertarians." Pew Research Center, 2014. http://www.pewresearch.org/fact-tank/2014/08/25/in-search-of-libertarians.

Ladd, Chris. "The Libertarian Civil Rights Paradox." *Forbes*, September 17, 2016. https://www.forbes.com/sites/chrisladd/2016/09/17/the-libertarian-civil-rights-paradox/#7bf531c4caeb.

"Land Use and Public Property." Libertarian Party of California. Accessed December 10, 2018. https://ca.lp.org/issue/land-use-and-public-property.

Merced, Alex. "Monetary Policy and Inequality." BeingLibertarian.com, December 8, 2015. https://beinglibertarian.com/monetary-policy-and-inequality.

Paul, Ron. *Liberty Defined: 50 Essential Issues That Affect Our Freedom*. New York: Grand Central Publishing, 2011.

Rothbard, Murray. *For a New Liberty, The Libertarian Manifesto*. London, UK: Macmillan Publishers, 1973.

——. *What Has Government Done to Our Money?* Auburn, AL: Ludwig von Mises Institute, 1963.

Sachs, Jeffrey. "Libertarian Illusions." *Huffington Post*, January 1, 2012. http://www.earth.columbia.edu/sitefiles/file/Sachs%20Writing/2012/HuffPost_2012_LibertarianIllusions_01_15_12.pdf.

Scandlen, Greg. "The Supreme Court's Reign of Terror, 1937–1944." *Federalist*, December 4, 2014. http://thefederalist.com/2014/12/04/the-supreme-courts-reign-of-terror-1937-1944.

Smith, Adam, and Edwin Cannan. *Inquiry into the Nature and Causes of the Wealth of Nations*. New York: Modern Library, 1994.

"2018 Platform." Libertarian Party, July 2018. https://www.lp.org/platform.

Index

Page numbers in **boldface** refer to images.

Tempra Board is a writer living in Northern California. She has spent the past twenty years as a grant writer for nonprofit organizations in the United States and Canada, including health and human services, arts, social justice, and environmental organizations. Board enjoys following the fascinating and sometimes frustrating world of American politics.